Great Answer Book

Compiled by Anna Pansini
Illustrated by Janice Kinnealy

Troll Associates

Library of Congress Cataloging-in-Publication Data

Pansini, Anna.
   Great answer book: I wonder why / compiled by Anna Pansini;
illustrated by Janice Kinnealy.
      p.   cm.
   Summary: School children wonder about the answers to science
questions, such as why beavers build dams and why hair turns gray,
and about the answers to everyday questions, such as why doughnuts
have holes.
   ISBN 0-8167-2308-7 (lib. bdg.)   ISBN 0-8167-2309-5 (pbk.)
   1. Children's questions and answers.   [1. Questions and answers.]
I. Kinnealy, Janice, ill.   II. Title.
AG195.P36   1991
031.02—dc20   90-44452

If you are like most kids, you wonder about many things. You have plenty of questions, and you want answers to them—fast. So we challenged kids all across America to come up with the answers to the questions they wonder about most. The response was tremendous!

The very best questions and answers were compiled and put into this book, and two others—*"I Wonder Why"* and *Kids' Question & Answer Book.* Each is filled with over 100 questions and answers on topics that kids are curious about.

Each contestant's name appears under the answers. Each book contains an alphabetical listing of winners, along with age or grade, school, and school address.

Finally, we'd like to thank all the students who entered the contest and the teachers who encouraged them.

Brighten your future

I wonder why kids have to go to school...

You have to go to school to get a good education, so you can get a good job and make lots of money. Then you can become rich and famous and answer questions that you never thought you could. Going to school can help with most any job. For example, if you are a journalist, you would have to know how to write; and if you are a musician, you would have to know how to read music. If you did not go to school, you would not be able to do any of these things. Besides, if your parents found out, they would be pretty mad!

Kristin Camp

I wonder why I do so bad in spelling...

I think it's because I don't study as I should, or maybe it's because I dislike memorizing things. All I know is I only got one hundred once. I wish there were no spelling tests, then I'd get plenty of rest and school would be the best.

Sam Johnson

I quit!

I wonder why people quit school...

They probably don't like the food served in the cafeteria. Or maybe they don't like the classroom they're in. Maybe they quit because school isn't as fun as playing all day long. Or maybe they quit because they don't like the principal or the way their teacher dresses. Well, whatever their reason, quitting school means your life is over before it has begun. So make the right choice—stay in school.

Chrissy Perkins

I wonder why people lose their hair...

Baldness results when the hair on a person's scalp is no longer replaced after it falls out. It occurs more frequently in men than in women. It depends largely on heredity. But other factors, including scalp diseases and exposure to radiation, can also cause baldness.

Tristan Santos

ouch!

WOW!

100,000

I wonder how many hairs are on a person's head...

Some people have as many as half a million. Most of us have about 100,000 hairs on our head. How did anyone ever count that many?

Kaysha Streich

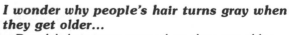

I wonder why people's hair turns gray when they get older...

People's hair turns gray when they get older because they produce less melanin as they get older. Melanin is a pigment that determines the color of their hair.

Sam Franklin

I wonder why I am so tall...

I think it would be better to be short. It's awful being the tallest kid in class. Maybe I'm tall because my dad is 6'2". But whatever the reason, I hate being tall. I think girls should be shorter than boys, but instead, I'm 5'4" and all the boys and girls are shorter than I am. I wonder if I will get any taller. I hope not! If I keep growing, I'm going to be a giant. I don't like being tall. It's absolutely terrible. I wish there was a way for me to shrink.

Trena Shea Bell

I wonder why boys like girls...

Because boys think girls are pretty! Probably also because liking girls is in style. Maybe boys think girls have pretty hair or pretty faces. Or maybe boys think girls are cool. Maybe boys like the clothes girls wear, or something like that. Maybe it's...I don't really know. Maybe boys just think girls are different. Maybe that's the way boys work!

Brianna Sanders

I wonder why my little sister follows me around all the time...

No matter where I go, my little sister follows me. I ask her why she follows me, and she says, "I don't know." Sometimes I ask her not to follow me, but she still does. Every time I go somewhere, she goes too. I guess she follows me because she likes me. I think she won't follow me as much when she gets older. So I guess I could put up with my "little shadow" a little longer.

Mindy McBride

I wonder why I am so short...

Sometimes I wish I was tall, and sometimes I'm glad I'm short. Being short can be fun, but I don't like it when people tease me about being short. One nice thing about being short is that you can run faster than tall people. Some people think tall people look funny, but I don't. Besides it doesn't matter how short or tall you are, what counts is how short or tall you feel.

Leslie Ann Webster

I wonder why grandparents "baby" their grandchildren...

It's strange that grandparents "baby" us instead of their own children. It's not that I don't like it. I do. I gets lots of very nice toys from my grandparents. Grandparents probably "baby" us because they miss having little kids of their own. Their kids have grown up, and now they have us to "baby."

Sarah Meier

I wonder why boys always act so dumb...

I guess it's because they like to show off, and like to impress people. They think they are cool because they can ride skateboards and pop wheelies on their bikes. They act like they have to entertain everybody in the whole wide world all the time.

Leslie Nichols

7

I wonder why you get dizzy when you spin around...

When you spin around, the fluid in your ear, which controls motion, begins to slosh around. When this fluid sloshes around, the hairs in the semicircular canals move in all directions, which sends a message of what is happening to the brain. After you stop spinning around, the fluid and hairs in your ear continue to move around for a while. That is why it looks like your surroundings are still moving around in circles after you've stopped.

Amanda Tate

I wonder why you can't get chicken pox more than once...

When people get sick, their white blood cells begin fighting the harmful germs in their bodies. One of the ways the white cells fight is by making germ-killers, or antibodies, for each sickness.

If a person catches chicken pox, his or her white cells make chicken pox antibodies. After that person gets well, these chicken pox antibodies stay in the blood and keep killing any chicken pox germs that may get in. That is why a person can't catch chicken pox twice. The person becomes immune to chicken pox.

Nicole Thornton

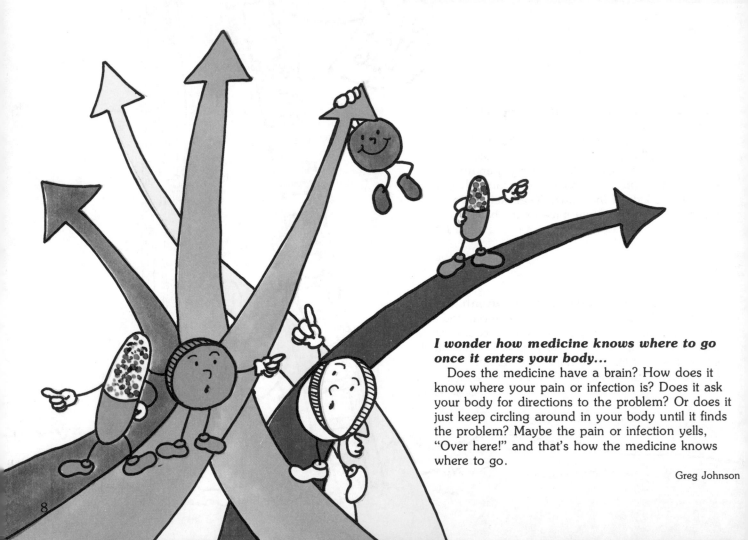

I wonder how medicine knows where to go once it enters your body...

Does the medicine have a brain? How does it know where your pain or infection is? Does it ask your body for directions to the problem? Or does it just keep circling around in your body until it finds the problem? Maybe the pain or infection yells, "Over here!" and that's how the medicine knows where to go.

Greg Johnson

8

I wonder why your body temperature rises...

A person's normal body temperature is 98.6°F. A sick person's temperature may rise as high as 105°F. Chemical reactions in the muscles and glands are always producing heat. When we are well, the extra heat produced is lost during breathing and sweating. The balancing of heat produced and heat given off leaves us with a healthy temperature of 98.6°F.

There are many reasons why the body temperature rises. A heat stroke, exposure to heat, swelling, and toxic reaction are a few such reasons. The most common reason for a fever is the presence of infectious germs in the body. Poisons made by these germs affect the mechanisms in the body that control temperature. That is why the body's temperature rises.

John David Bookout

I wonder how you catch a cold...

Cold germs are so small that you cannot see them as they float about in the air. But these germs can get into your body through your nose. When a person with a cold sneezes, cold germs shoot out in all directions. They may get into your body and give you a cold, too. That is why when someone has a bad cold, people tell that person to cover his or her nose and mouth when sneezing. The best way to keep people from catching your cold is to stay in bed and away from other people.

Alonzo Williams

I wonder why coin banks are shaped like pigs...

Cookware in Europe was once made of dense orange clay called "pygg." As people began saving coins in jars made of this clay, the jars became known as "pygg jars." In the 19th century, an English potter was asked to make a "pygg" bank, but he made one shaped like a pig instead.

Lakesha Ridgele

I wonder why furniture makes creaking noises at night...

Furniture makes creaking noises because during the day the heat from the sun causes everything to expand a little, including furniture. At night, everything cools and shrinks. When furniture shrinks, it makes creaking noises.

Dina Macchia

I wonder why my eyes sometimes appear red on a flash picture when I look directly at the camera...

The pupils in my eyes appear to be red because the light from the flash reflects off of my eye and back out into the camera.

Alison Blakely

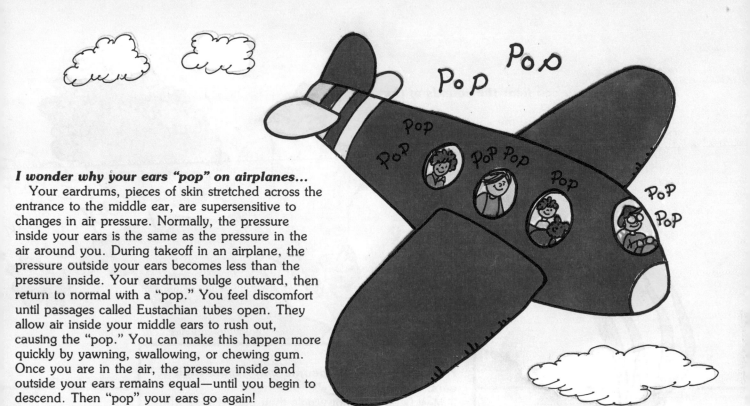

I wonder why your ears "pop" on airplanes...

Your eardrums, pieces of skin stretched across the entrance to the middle ear, are supersensitive to changes in air pressure. Normally, the pressure inside your ears is the same as the pressure in the air around you. During takeoff in an airplane, the pressure outside your ears becomes less than the pressure inside. Your eardrums bulge outward, then return to normal with a "pop." You feel discomfort until passages called Eustachian tubes open. They allow air inside your middle ears to rush out, causing the "pop." You can make this happen more quickly by yawning, swallowing, or chewing gum. Once you are in the air, the pressure inside and outside your ears remains equal—until you begin to descend. Then "pop" your ears go again!

Nicole Camboni

I wonder why I get goose bumps when I am cold...

Goose bumps are tiny bumps that form around each strand of hair. They are caused by the contraction, or pulling in, of tiny muscles which cause the hair to stand up. Since we have a very small amount of hair, or body fur, goose bumps do not do much for us. They provide us with little protection. Goose bumps are very useful for animals with a lot of hair or body fur because it causes their fur to puff out to form a warmer coat.

Nicole Roberts

11

I wonder why you can hear the sounds of the ocean in a seashell...

The sounds you hear are the sounds around you. The shell amplifies the sounds. The seashell's hollow body is really picking up sounds and making them louder. These sounds make you think of the ocean's roar.

Ben Griggs

Honk Honk Beep

Bang

I hear the Ocean

I wonder why some people can wiggle their ears...

Most people cannot wiggle their ears. Those who can are able to use muscles that are attached to their outer ears. Everybody has these muscles but not everybody can use them. Can you?

Amanda Storm

Onion Oil

I wonder why onions make people cry...

Have you ever watched someone cut an onion? Did you notice tears swelling up in his or her eyes? What is it about an onion that makes people cry?

Onions contain a mildly stimulating oil. This oil is readily released when the onion is cut. The oil lets off an odor that irritates the eyes, causing the tear glands to produce tears to wash the irritating odor from the eyes. This is why people cry when they cut an onion.

Tina Honeycutt

I wonder why you can see your breath on a cold day...

On most days, you cannot see your breath. But on some cold days, you can. When you exhale on a cold day, your breath forms a tiny white cloud. We are warm-blooded, and thus our body temperature is always around 98.6°F even though the temperature outside may be colder. So when we exhale on a cold day, our breath is much warmer than the air outside. When your warm breath mixes with the cold air outside, it forms water droplets, or water vapor. This is why you see a white cloud when you exhale on a cold day.

Patrick Lantry

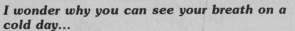

I wonder why people blush when they're embarrassed...

I think it's because they want to do something and they are either afraid to do it or afraid to tell a person that they like him or her. People also blush if they have been doing something good for a long time and someone finally notices them, or they do something wrong and everyone notices.

Christina Rae

I wonder why people's feet smell...

The skin on your feet is covered with tiny sweat glands that help you stay cool. Sweat glands ooze a watery liquid that contains salt and a chemical called urea. Urea causes your feet to smell. Your feet don't sweat any more than your hands or armpits do, but because your feet are usually wrapped in socks and shoes, the liquid has no way to escape. It just stays there and collects the whole day. So when you take your shoes and socks off at the end of the day, your feet will smell.

Blake Matheny

You Smell!

Yuck!

I wonder why doesn't a bird fall off of the branch while it's sleeping...

A bird's feet have a built-in locking device. The muscles and tendons that run the full length of its legs automatically pull its toes into a fist, or lock, when the bird sleeps.

Keri Hassel

I wonder why geese fly in a V-formation...

They fly in a V-formation because this flying formation makes it easier for them to break a trail through the wind. The lead bird breaks a trail through the air and all the other birds follow after it. This makes the job of flying much easier for the birds that follow in the V because it saves them energy and gives them a rest until they become the leader. Each bird takes a turn at being the leader.

Tobias Dawson

I wonder why fish don't sink and drown...

Fish don't sink because they have powerful body muscles and they have fins. Fish may have as many as five kinds of fins—the dorsal fins, the anal fins, the tail fin, the pelvic fins and the pectoral fin.

The dorsal fins and the anal fins keep the fish from rolling from side to side while swimming. The tail fin steers the fish through the water. The pelvic fins and the pectoral fins control fine movements of the fish. To help fish float in the water, they have gas-filled sacs called swim bladders inside their bodies. The amount of gas in the swim bladder is controlled by the fish. If the fish needs gas, the fish rises and if the fish has enough gas, it sinks.

Christopher Richardson

14

I wonder why spiders aren't caught in their own webs...

"Won't you come into my parlor?" said the spider to the fly. The tricky spider knows that once the fly lands on the web, it will not be able to escape and the spider will have a nice meal. But why does the sticky web only trap the fly and not the spider? Actually, the spider can be caught in its own web too. But this doesn't happen because the spider knows its way around its web. When the spider spins a web, it spins certain "safe" threads, which it can touch without getting "caught."

Sharon Nunez

I wonder why bats hang upside down...

There are several reasons why bats hang upside down. The most common reason is so they can start their winter's hibernation. When they start their hibernation, they wrap their wings snugly around themselves. As the winter's weather becomes colder, the bat's body temperature falls until it is close to the freezing mark. All its other body functions slow down as well until it becomes completely inactive. It will live through the winter on the food energy it has stored during the summer months of busy eating.

Robin Thornton

I wonder if snake charmers really charm snakes with their music...

No, snakes cannot be charmed by music. Snake charmers play music and cobras seem to dance to it, but they aren't really dancing to it because snakes cannot hear very well. A cobra can watch its victim carefully and imitate its victim's movements—that is what the snake does when it appears to move to the music. It is really just imitating the swaying of the snake charmer. A snake charmer takes a big chance when he excites a cobra because cobras have a poisonous, deadly venom. But some snake charmers know how to keep an excited cobra from actually striking. Other snake charmers remove the cobra's fangs so that they are completely safe.

Jennifer Radich

15

I wonder if sheep get cold when they get their wool sheared off...

Maybe they don't get cold because their fat keeps them warm. They usually get their wool sheared in the spring and summer. In the summer, they are probably glad to get their wool sheared off because it would be too hot. By the time their wool grows back, it will be winter and they will be glad to have it long.

Erica Ford

I wonder if birds can fly backwards...

Most birds can't, but a hummingbird can fly in any direction, including backwards. It can fly forwards, backwards, to either side, diagonally, and it even can stand still in the air. The hummingbird is the only bird that can fly backwards.

Shannon Munns

I wonder why raccoons wash their food...

There may be some truth to the stories that raccoons wash their food before eating it, but this habit does not indicate cleanliness since the water they dip it in can be dirty. Actually, it seems that the raccoon just likes to wet its food before it eats it.

Kerry Hartness

16

I wonder why flamingos stand on one leg...

Flamingos and other wading birds stand on one foot. They do this so it is easier for them to hunt for food in the water. By standing on just one leg, the shadow it casts in the water resembles a tree—one leg appears as a tree trunk and its body looks like the top of a tree. When the bird does this, fish see the shadow, think it's a tree and swim by without caution. That's how flamingos hunt for food.

Kyle McNerney

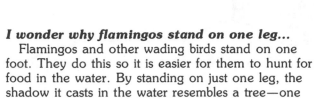

I wonder why flamingos are pink...

It's not because they were born that way. Flamingos have to eat special food to keep their color. The food contains carotene which turns their feathers pink. If it wasn't for the food they eat, flamingos would be totally white.

Monica Steen

I wonder why hummingbirds don't fly like other birds...

A hummingbird flies almost like a helicopter. It can fly up and down, backwards and forwards, left and right at very fast speeds. The hummingbird can stay in one spot for a very long time to get nectar out of a flower to eat. The hummingbird flaps its wings about 60-70 times a second. That is how a hummingbird flies.

Anna Steffen

17

I wonder why polar bears don't slip on ice...
Polar bears don't slip on ice because they have little hairs on the bottom of their feet and that keeps them from slipping on the ice.

Karen Lewis

I wonder what a Kodiak bear is...
A Kodiak bear is a large, powerful animal. While most bears eat fish, the Kodiak bear is the best fish catcher. It is one kind of the Great Alaskan Brown Bear. It is about 9 feet long. Although these bears mostly eat fish, they will eat almost anything that is available. And while the female may look weaker than the male, a mother bear can tear apart any male bear that gets near her cubs.

Shannon Seda

I wonder how a crocodile keeps its teeth clean...
People use toothpaste and a toothbrush to clean their teeth. But some crocodiles have a bird friend who cleans their teeth and their mouth. This bird is not afraid of a crocodile at all. It hops right into the crocodile's huge mouth—and pecks away at tiny bits of food stuck in the crocodile's teeth. Somehow the crocodile knows that the bird is helping it, so it keeps its mouth wide open.

Traneka Adams

I wonder why turtles walk so slowly...
Because they have little feet.

Melinda Avila

I wonder why some gecko lizards can walk across a ceiling and up walls...
The gecko lizard has sticky pads and hairs on the bottom of its feet. This allows some geckos to walk across ceilings and up walls. So when you're in your house, remember to watch out for the gecko lizard!

Holly Thomas

I wonder why snakes don't close their eyes...
Actually, snakes do close their eyes. But their eyelids are clear, so you can't see them. When enemies approach a sleeping snake, the snake's eyelids are shut but because they are clear, the enemy thinks the snake's eyes are open and it is awake. A snake that is awake is not easy to attack, so the enemy leaves the snake alone.

Cheryl Rogers

19

I wonder why rabbits have white puffy tails...
I think rabbits have white puffy tails because they are supposed to be cute. Besides, they are the only animals that wouldn't look silly with a white puffy tail. Imagine how funny a horse would look with a white puffy tail.

Edith Dabros

I wonder why elephants are gray...
Because they feel so sad. They are sad because they are too huge to see their own feet.

Jason Lewis

I wonder why a shark has to swim its whole life, even while it sleeps, without ever stopping...
A shark has to swim its whole life without stopping because it does not have a swim bladder to allow it to float when it is not moving. Moving through the water allows water to flow into its gills so it can breathe. If it stops swimming, it will sink and suffocate and die.

Sunner Soo-Hoo

How Gray I Am

20

I wonder if fish sleep...

When fish get very still, they're asleep. They won't close their eyes like people do because they don't have eyelids. It's not exactly the type of sleep that humans get, but many scientists would call it a form of sleep.

Natalie Washington

I wonder how polar bears stay so warm in such cold climates...

The sun's rays pass through the bear's hair and warm the air in the bear's fur. The warm air is then trapped in between the hair. Heat that is absorbed is trapped in thick rolls of fat under the skin. The polar bear's skin acts like a wet suit in the water, so it can stay warm in water too.

Emily Norton

I wonder how long a giraffe's tongue is...

About 21 inches long.

Julie Ivy

I wonder if ground hogs really can predict the weather...

No, ground hogs cannot predict the weather. However, the ground hog, also known as the woodchuck, hibernates all winter underground in a hole. Legend has it that on February 2nd of each year, Ground-hog Day, the ground hog will come out of its hole. If it is cloudy and the ground hog cannot see its shadow, the cold days of winter are over and spring will arrive shortly. If the ground hog sees its shadow and goes back into its hole, we will have about 6 more weeks of winter.

This legend about the ground hog is well known, but there really is no truth to it because ground hogs will stay underground until the weather warms up enough for them to come out, which may happen before, on, or after February 2nd. Once the ground hog does come out of its hole, it doesn't look for its shadow. Instead it just goes about its business, which is not predicting the weather.

Elizabeth Lesser

I wonder why animals have tails...

Animals use their tails in many ways. The tails of water animals help them steer in the water.

Land animals use their tails for a variety of things. Squirrels use their tails to keep their balance when they jump from tree branch to tree branch. Cows and horses use their tails to swat at flies. Kangaroos use their tails to balance when they jump. Monkeys and opossums use their tails for grasping things. Beavers use their tails to help them swim and warn other beavers of danger.

Eric Venet

I wonder why birds build nests...

Because they need a home to keep their babies safe and warm.

Peggy Bostic

Home Sweet Home

I wonder why cheetahs have spots...

Cheetahs have spots as protective coloration. Protective coloration helps many animals hide from their enemies. When a cheetah lies down, its fur blends in with the ground and the dark spots look like shadows. The cheetah uses its protective coloration to fool an enemy.

Katie Martin

I wonder why the cheetah runs so fast...

Unlike other cats who tend to lie in wait for their prey and pounce on it with a single leap or a short attack, cheetahs stalk their prey and then race after it for some distance. In a short sprint, cheetahs can easily overtake their prey. But if their prey gets a good start, the cheetah can drop out of the chase exhausted because it only has short-lived energy for a quick burst.

Roberto Quezada

I wonder how basketball started...

Basketball is the only major sport played today that began in America. A minister created the game in 1891. The minister wanted a safe game for young boys to play, which did not allow pushing or forcibly touching the other players. He wanted a game that all children could play safely together regardless of strength or weight (unlike football).

He decided that the object of the game would be to see who could throw the most number of throws landing the large, lightweight ball in a peach basket which hung from each end of the gymnasium where the game was to be held. The problem was that each time the ball landed in the peach basket, someone would have to crawl up on a ladder to get it down. So open hoops were used instead of baskets for the ball to drop through.

The hoop was put on a pole and a backboard was later devised. Obviously the name "basketball" was derived from the fact that the ball was thrown into a peach basket. The hoops and net are still referred to today as the "basket."

Kristen Puvalowski

I wonder why runners start at different positions in a race and not all at one starting line...

Because the lanes on the inside of a circular track cover less ground than on the outside. So in order to be fair to all runners, they start at different positions so they will all have the same distance to run to reach the finish line.

Fatin Sabur

I wonder why swimmers wear swim caps in competition...

There are several reasons why swimmers wear swim caps in competition. First, a cap designates which team you swim with so the spectators will know without actually having to know you. Caps also make it easier for coaches to spot members of their team in the water. Second, a cap keeps your head warm. It is very important to keep your body heat in. Third, a cap cuts down on water resistance. It helps you move a little faster in the water. Fourth, it helps your goggles stay in place. And fifth, it helps protect your ears.

Sean Pruitt

I wonder why the Statue of Liberty was built...

The actual name for the statue is "Liberty Enlightening the World." It was given to the United States as a gift from the people of France to celebrate the 100th anniversary of the signing of the Declaration of Independence. "Liberty" stands at the gateway of the New World to welcome everyone who is looking for a better life in our country.

Lauren Hoaglano

I wonder why there is wind...

Wind is caused by the uneven heating of the sun. Cold air moves to warmer places. So when there is warm air in one place and cold air in another, the cold air moves to where the warm air is and creates wind. During the day, coastal land gets warmer than ocean water, so the wind blows from the ocean to the land causing ocean breezes. During the night, the land quickly loses its heat, which causes wind to blow from the land to the ocean. That is why there is wind on Earth.

Derek Hudson

I wonder why we get report cards in school...

So parents can see their child's strengths and abilities. They challenge students to try harder and do their best. It also shows areas where you may need improvement. It's a written record of your progress.

Heather Knappenberger

I wonder why you get something on your fingers after you hold a butterfly or moth...

People who touch the wings of a butterfly or moth get something that looks like dust on their fingers. The dust is actually tiny scales that grow in rows on the butterfly's wings and pattern its color. They come off when you touch them. The scales also account for the scientific name for butterflies and moths, which is Lepidoptera or "scaly winged."

April Bush

I wonder why bees make honey...

Making honey is an important part of a bee's life. While they are making the honey, they are also feeding themselves a source of protein. The protein comes from the pollen they get from the flowers. Honey is a great source of energy for bees.

Steven Romej

I wonder how fleas jump...

When a flea jumps, it is almost in a somersault position. One pair of legs is above its body to help it keep its balance in the air.

Luke James Kennedy

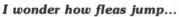

Boing!

Boing!

I wonder how grasshoppers hop...

Grasshoppers hop because they have long legs with large thighs that are very strong. Therefore, they are able to jump far distances many times their own length. They also have wings which they use only to fly short distances. Some people have seen them jump, but not often.

Rosie Gonzalez

I wonder why leaves change colors...

Leaves are such a pretty sight.
Especially in the fall when they are colorfully bright.
Every spring, the buds appear on the trees.
The buds are the beginning of new leaves.
For new leaves to grow,
They need sunlight, air, water, and chlorophyll.
Chlorophyll keeps the leaves healthy and green.
But all the pretty colors cannot be seen.
Remember when you see a leaf,
The true colors are underneath.
In the fall as the chlorophyll disappears,
The hidden colors start to appear.
Red, yellow, orange and brown—
All these beautiful colors can be found.
So remember when you see a leaf,
To think of all the colors underneath.

Nicole Rasmussen

I wonder why trees have bark...

A tree has bark so it can protect its inner layers.
Tree bark works like your skin does.

The inner part of a tree's bark consists of a tube that keeps food and water circulating throughout the tree. If a little piece of bark is torn off, it could damage the whole tree because it will cut off the food and water supply to other parts of the tree, which may die. So bark plays a very important part in the life of a tree.

Chris Pike

I wonder why the ozone is important to our planet...

Ozone is a form of oxygen with a strong cleaning agent and a chemically active gas. Ozone was discovered by a German chemist, Christian Friedrich Schonbein, in 1840. Ozone is important to our planet because it prevents very high energy radiation from the sun from striking the earth's atmosphere. Fluorocarbons from Earth rise up into the earth's atmosphere and gradually reduce the ozone.

Carolina Padilla

I wonder why evergreens are always green...

Most trees are green only during the summer. But certain trees, such as pines and spruces, stay green all year round. The leaves that change color and drop off do so for good reason. These kinds of leaves cannot stand up to icy winds and freezing cold temperatures. In self-defense, the tree makes its leaves change color, dry out and die. Once the harsh winter is over, the tree grows a complete new set of leaves. Evergreens, however, are designed to stand up to severe weather. Their waxy, needle-like leaves hold their water and so do not dry out. These sturdy little leaves can also survive blasts of winter winds. Most evergreens keep their leaves all year round. Many of them keep their leaves for several years. And they always grow new leaves before shedding their old ones. Since they look green all the time, they're called evergreens!

Kristee Lawson

I wonder why flowers smell so good...

In most cases, the odor of a flower comes from oily substances in the petals. Strong odors, like bright colors, attract insects.

Margarite Nathe

I wonder why some plants eat animals...

Carnivorous plants have special leaves to trap and digest small animals and insects. By eating animals and insects, these plants absorb nutrients they can't get from the soil. Carnivorous plants lure insects and animals by a sticky substance or different colors on their leaves. The plant then traps them and digests what it has captured. Some carnivorous plants are the Butterwort, Pitcher plant, Venus's-flytrap and Sundew.

Erin Prendergast

29

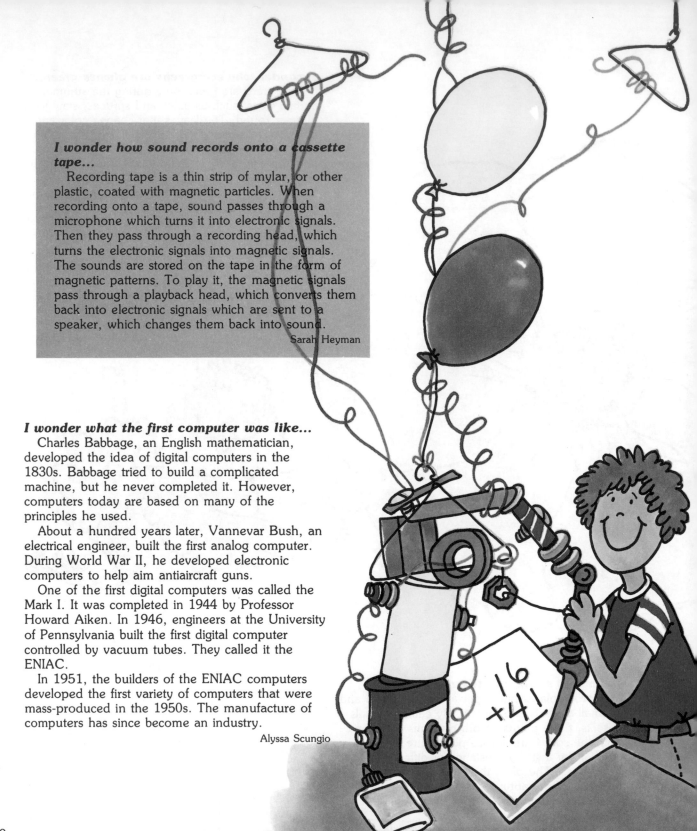

I wonder how sound records onto a cassette tape...

Recording tape is a thin strip of mylar, or other plastic, coated with magnetic particles. When recording onto a tape, sound passes through a microphone which turns it into electronic signals. Then they pass through a recording head, which turns the electronic signals into magnetic signals. The sounds are stored on the tape in the form of magnetic patterns. To play it, the magnetic signals pass through a playback head, which converts them back into electronic signals which are sent to a speaker, which changes them back into sound.

Sarah Heyman

I wonder what the first computer was like...

Charles Babbage, an English mathematician, developed the idea of digital computers in the 1830s. Babbage tried to build a complicated machine, but he never completed it. However, computers today are based on many of the principles he used.

About a hundred years later, Vannevar Bush, an electrical engineer, built the first analog computer. During World War II, he developed electronic computers to help aim antiaircraft guns.

One of the first digital computers was called the Mark I. It was completed in 1944 by Professor Howard Aiken. In 1946, engineers at the University of Pennsylvania built the first digital computer controlled by vacuum tubes. They called it the ENIAC.

In 1951, the builders of the ENIAC computers developed the first variety of computers that were mass-produced in the 1950s. The manufacture of computers has since become an industry.

Alyssa Scungio

I wonder how a jet engine works...

Air is sucked into the engine and squeezed by fans until it is under great pressure. It then mixes with a special fuel, and the fuel explodes. The exhaust gases from the explosion are forced out and this thrusts the plane forward.

Matthew Eric Drum

I wonder how an automobile works...

When you turn the key in the ignition, electricity starts to flow from the battery to the motor. The motor spins the crankshaft, which makes the pistons in the cylinders move up and down. The battery also sends electricity to the distributor, which sends it to the spark plug. The turning crankshaft operates the fuel pump, which takes the gasoline from the fuel tank and sends it to the carburetor. Here the gasoline is mixed with air. The pistons draw the fuel into the cylinders, where it is ignited by the spark plugs. Then the pistons move up and down, turning the crankshaft which turns the transmission. The transmission turns some gears and turns the drive shaft. The drive shaft turns the wheels which makes the automobile move.

David Fuller

How Cars Work

Planes

31

We hit there last week!

I wonder why lightning will only strike a spot once...

Lightning is a huge, electrical spark in the sky. Most people believe that a bolt of lightning will only strike a spot once. However, scientists believe it can strike a spot more than once, but that is very unlikely. The possibility of the same exact physical circumstances occurring in nature more than once is highly unlikely. But it can happen.

Mitchell Schlesinger

I wonder why I see my reflection when I look in a mirror...

When you stand in front of a mirror, light bounces off you and passes through the glass to the shiny layer behind the glass. When the light hits this shiny material, it bounces straight back. This is why your image is reflected in a mirror.

Nicholas Koenig

I wonder what asteroids are...

An asteroid is an extremely small planet that revolves around the sun. They are also called minor planets or planetoids. Asteroids mostly travel between Mars and Jupiter. There are thousands of asteroids that we know of, and new ones are being discovered all the time. There are 30,000 asteroids which are bright enough for us to see.

Brad Wilson

I wonder why there are comets...

A comet is a heavenly body in orbit around the sun that looks like a star with a long tail. There are many comets in the solar system, but most of them are too small to be noticeable. In ancient times, the large bright comets were thought to be signs from heaven, and they caused widespread panic. The British astronomer Edmund Halley suggested that three famous comets that had appeared in 1531, 1607, and 1682 were really the same. Using this theory, he predicted that the comet would come again in 1759—and it did. This comet is now known as Halley's Comet. It appears every 75 or 76 years. The slight variation in its orbit is caused by the gravitation of the planets. Comets travel in very eccentric orbits, sometimes far outside the solar system but sometimes closer to the sun than the earth is. Many comets are found by amateur astronomers and are sometimes named after them.

Stacy Long

I wonder what the sun is made of and how heavy it is...

The sun is a glowing ball of hot gases. These gases are made up of many of the same chemical elements we find in the crust of the earth. The most common elements in the sun are hydrogen, helium, calcium, sodium, magnesium, and iron.

The gases at the center of the sun are dense and heavy, but the gases at the surface are much lighter. For its size, the sun is much lighter than the earth. The sun is very big. It weighs 331,950 times more than the earth.

Amanda Star Kornitz

I wonder what quasars are...

"Quasar" is a shortened form of "quasi-stellar radio source." Quasars are sometimes mistaken for stars. Even though they are the size of our solar system, they cannot be seen with the naked eye because they are about 10 billion light years away from the earth. Quasars are extremely bright objects. They can be one trillion times brighter than the sun. They give off enormous amounts of energy in the form of visible light, ultraviolet light, infrared rays, x-rays, and sometimes radio waves. Quasars were first discovered in 1963 by astronomers at the Palomar Observatory in California.

Jeffrey Han

I wonder what a falling star is...

The bright flash of light you see streaking across the night sky isn't really a star. It's a piece of rock called a meteor. A meteor gets very hot as it falls through the air around the earth. The meteor becomes so hot it glows. These "shooting stars" usually burn up before they hit the ground.

Christie Crane

I wonder why stars are so small when we look at them...

The sun is the closest star to us. The other billions of stars are so far away that they appear to be no more than pinpoints of light—even through powerful telescopes. There are more than 200 billion billion stars. In spite of their appearance, stars are enormous objects. The sun is only a medium-sized star, but its diameter is more than 100 times the diameter of the earth. The largest stars would more than fill the space between the earth and the sun. Such stars have a diameter that is about 1,000 times as large as the sun's.

Sean Stock

I wonder why a hamburger is called a hamburger since there is no ham in it...

There is no ham at all in a hamburger. It's made of ground beef. Americans think of hamburgers as an American food, but they really came from Germany. Long ago, many German people came to America to live. With them, they brought a lot of recipes for their favorite foods. One of these foods was a kind of meat ball made of ground beef. These meat balls were supposed to have been invented in the German city of Hamburg, so they became known as Hamburg-ers.

Amy Brogan

I wonder why your stomach growls...

When your stomach growls, your stomach muscles are pushing around the air inside your stomach. It can also growl when you have just eaten because your stomach muscles move around to mix the food you have just eaten with special juices. They also move around the air you have swallowed with your food.

Brooke Bonner

I wonder how shoo-fly pie got its name...

There are no shoes or flies in it. A long time ago, people used to put their pies out on their windowsills. Flies would swarm to the pie, and the people would have to shoo the flies away from it. Now it is called shoo-fly pie.

Nicole Weaver

I wonder why the chocolates in a box of chocolates come in different shapes...

Some companies do this so you can tell what is in the center of each chocolate without having to break it open or bite it first. Usually squares are caramels, rectangular chocolates are nougat, ovals are nuts, and circular chocolates are cream-filled.

Katie Sullivan

I wonder how frankfurters came to be...

Frankfurters were named after Frankfurt, Germany. These sausages were probably first made in Germany during the Middle Ages. German and American vendors selling cooked frankfurters supposedly called them "hot dachshund sausages" because they resembled the long-bodied dog. Later the term "hot dog" came to be used.

Fritz Van de Kamp

I wonder why doughnuts have holes in them...

So they will cook completely through in a short time. If they didn't have holes, the outer part of the doughnut would be cooked while the center would still need to be cooked more.

Bethany James

I wonder what causes the greenhouse effect...

The greenhouse effect got its name because the earth's atmosphere acts like the glass or plastic roof and walls of a greenhouse. Sunlight enters a greenhouse through the glass or plastic and heats the plants. The roof and walls slow down the escape of the heat. The earth's atmosphere allows most of the sunlight that reaches it to pass through and heat the earth's surface. The earth sends the heat energy back into the atmosphere. But certain gases in the atmosphere absorb it while other gases grow warm and send heat energy back to the earth, causing temperatures on the surface to rise more.

Jennifer Treadwell

I wonder what hail is...

Hail is made up of small lumps of ice that sometimes fall to the earth during thunderstorms. These icy stones are formed inside the thunderclouds. The tops of high thunderclouds are always very cold. Down near the bottom of these clouds, the air is much warmer. Raindrops get blown down with many layers of ice on them. The icy stones, or hailstones, can be many different sizes. The biggest known hailstone was over 17 inches around.

Heather Colletti

I wonder why beaches have sand...

Beach sand primarily comes from the action of rivers and streams as they wear away rocks. Eroded particles of granite are washed into the sea where currents and waves carry them ashore as grains of sand. Most grains of sand are light-colored bits of quartz and other minerals. In Hawaii, volcanic rock is broken down and black sand is created in some spots. Some sand consists of tiny, broken bits of shell and coral. Not all beaches are sandy—some have pebbles or cobblestones.

Lindsay Harris

I wonder why mothers and fathers get gray hair...

Because their children give them a hard time, and because they are getting old.

Katie Zabinsky

I wonder why some people are right-handed and some are left-handed...

Each side of your brain controls muscles on the opposite side of your body. Usually the left side of the brain is more powerful, or dominant, than the right side, which means you will have better control over the muscles on the right side of your body.

If the right side of your brain is more powerful, you will be left-handed and have better control over the muscles on the left side of your body.

When both sides of your brain are about equal, you are ambidextrous and can use one hand as well as the other.

Chrissie Marino

I wonder why learning a foreign language is so important...

There are many important reasons for learning a foreign language. Among them are the following: 1) Learning a foreign language increases your range of communication. For example, if you only speak English, you can communicate with about 450,000,000 people in the United States, Canada, Great Britain, and other English-speaking countries. But if you speak Spanish as well, you could also speak to the 300,000,000 Spanish-speaking people in the world. 2) By learning another language, you gain knowledge of the customs and ways of life of other nations. For example, while learning French, you can learn about how the French live, behave, and think.

Natalie Johnson

I wonder how language began...

No one knows when or how language began, but there are many theories. According to many theories, language first was one of two things. Maybe it was an imitation of natural sounds, such as groans and barks, or it might have been an accompaniment to gestures or other body movements. There was no way of recording language when it began.

Janie Jones

41

I wonder how the idea for Santa Claus started...

The idea for Santa Claus developed from stories about a real person named St. Nicholas. According to tradition, he lived in Patara, which is now Turkey. When he was 19, he became a priest. He once aided a poor nobleman and his three daughters by throwing three bags of money through their window. The legend of St. Nicholas bringing gifts probably developed from this story.

Michelle Schneider

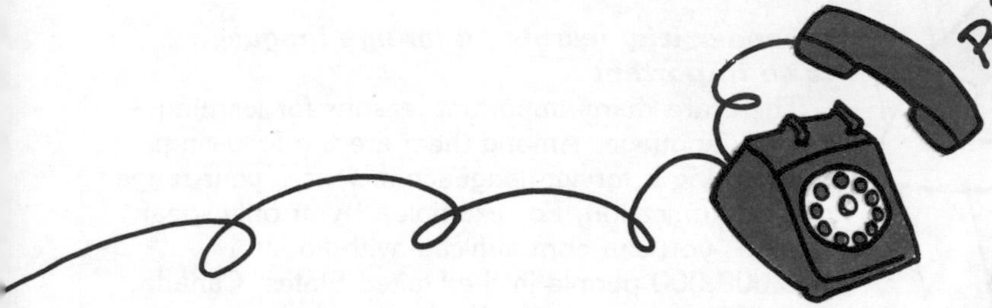

I wonder why there is a Mother's Day and a Father's Day...

These are special days for appreciating our parents and all they do for us. They buy us food, fix dinner, buy clothes, take us on trips, help us with schoolwork, wake us up in the morning for school, make our breakfast, take care of our pets for us, and more. I love my parents very much because of all the things they do for me. I think it's important to have Mother's Day and Father's Day so we can show parents how much we appreciate them. Parents are the most important people in the whole world.

Matt Howell

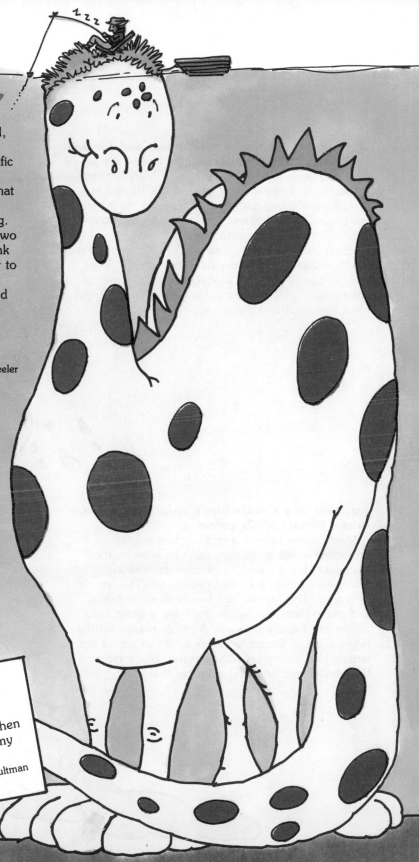

I wonder if there really is a Loch Ness Monster...

In a lake called Loch Ness in northern Scotland, people believe there is a monster. It is called the Loch Ness Monster, or Nessie for short. Its scientific name is *Nessiteras rhombopterys*. With this classification, it can be protected by a British law that safeguards rare animals until it is studied further. People describe it as measuring up to 30 feet long. The creature is believed to have flippers, one or two humps, and a long thin neck. Some scientists think Nessie may be related to a dinosaur-like reptile or to a modern sea animal—Nessie may be in the manatee or seal family. Scientists have investigated the bottom of the lake with sonar to detect underwater objects. They have discovered large moving bodies in the lake. Could it—or they—be the monster or monsters of Loch Ness?

John Wheeler

I wonder what E.S.P. is...

E.S.P. stands for extrasensory perception. *Extra* means outside of. *Sensory* means of the senses. *Perception* means being aware of. So E.S.P. means being aware of things outside of your first five senses, which are sight, hearing, touch, taste, and smell.

Extrasensory perception is sometimes called "the sixth sense." It is when a person knows what another person is going to say or do, or what will happen in the future. It is also when a person can read another person's mind, or know another person's thoughts, without a word being spoken.

E.S.P. has been tested, but not proven.

Sherry Deckman

I wonder why I never, ever have any clean white socks...

Maybe there's an enormous sock monster that lives under my bed. In the middle of the night when everyone's asleep, it comes out and eats up all my clean white socks.

Kriss Hultman

I wonder why beavers build dams and canals...

Beavers build dams because they need a place to live and store food. They use logs, branches, and rocks stuck together with mud to build dams in small lakes. They use mud and stones for the base of the dam. Their dams are built from the bottom of the water up to the surface of the water.

Beavers also build canals so they can move logs to their dams or lodges easily and quickly. Their canals can run from a wooded area to a lake or river bank, or they may cut across a piece of land that sticks out into the water.

John Stuck

I wonder why a male bird's colors are brighter than a female bird's colors...

Most people believe a bird's colors are for protection—that is, so they can't be seen by their enemies. This is called "protective coloration." Which bird needs the most protection? The female, of course. The female bird has to sit on the eggs and hatch them, so nature gave her a duller color so she can't easily be seen. Another reason for the bright color of the male bird is so it can attract the female bird during breeding season. Many male birds have their brightest colors at that time.

Tiffany Shorter

I wonder why an octopus sprays out ink...

An octopus has a small sac of ink in its head. When the octopus is scared, it sprays ink out of its sac. The ink forms a dark black cloud in the water in front of its attacker so it can't see. Meanwhile, the octopus sneaks away from its attacker.

James Stalls

I wonder what makes the electricity in electric eels...

More than half of the electric eel's body is arranged somewhat like an automobile battery. It has rows and rows of small, thin plates with a liquid around each one. In a battery, the plates are made of metal. In an eel, they are made of living tissue, something like muscle. To get a strong electric current from several batteries, you connect them with copper wire. An eel's electric parts are connected in the same way. Living cords called nerves take the place of wires. The eel can make an electric current strong enough to stun a man. Scientists have managed to light electric bulbs with it.

Ami Holcomb

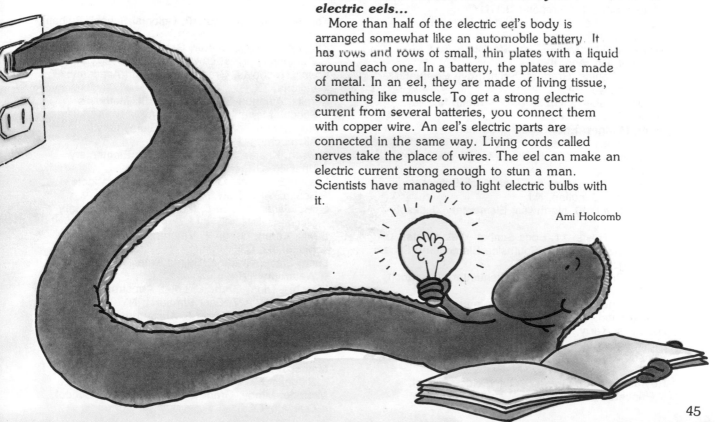

A Special Thanks To:

Adams, Traneka, Grade 4, Unadilla Elementary, Unadilla, GA

Avila, Melinda, Grade 4, St. Catherine School, Somerville, MA

Bell, Trena Shea, Grade 6, Taylor County Elementary, Campbellsville, KY

Blakely, Alison, Grade 4, Morgan School, Beloit, WI

Bonner, Brooke, Grade 4, Schulenburg Elementary, Schulenburg, TX

Bookout, John David, 11, Chalkville Elementary, Birmingham, AL

Bostic, Peggy, Grade 5, Gap Mills School, Gap Mills, WV

Brogan, Amy, Grade 4, C.W. Rice Elementary, Northumberland, PA

Bush, April, Grade 4, Sand Fork Elementary, Sand Fork, WV

Camboni, Nicole, Grade 4, Morgan School, Beloit, WI

Camp, Kristin, Grade 4, Swanton Elementary, Swanton, VT

Colletti, Heather, Grade 5, St. Benedict Joseph Labre School, Richmond Hill, NY

Crane, Christie, Grade 4, Unadilla Elementary, Unadilla, GA

Dabros, Edith, Grade 5, St. Stanislaus B. & M. School, Chicago, IL

Dawson, Tobias, Grade 4, Selinsgrove Elementary, Selinsgrove, PA

Deckman, Sherry, Grade 6, E.F. Smith Middle School, York, PA

Drum, Matthew Eric, Grade 4, Selinsgrove Elementary, Selinsgrove, PA

Ford, Erica, Grade 6, Herbert Marcus Elementary, Dallas, TX

Franklin, Sam, Grade 5, Dutch Neck School, Princeton Junction, NJ

Fuller, David, 10, Northwest Elementary, Jackson, MI

Gonzalez, Rosie, 11, Boos School, Westminster, CA

Griggs, Ben, Grade 4, Southside Elementary, Siloam Springs, AR

Han, Jeffrey, 11, Allamuchy Elementary, Allamuchy, NJ

Harris, Lindsay, Grade 5, Meyer Intermediate, Richmond, TX

Hartness, Kerry, Grade 5, Monticello Intermediate, Monticello, AR

Hassel, Keri, 11, Allamuchy Elementary, Allamuchy, NJ

Heyman, Sarah, Grade 5, Dutch Neck School, Princeton Junction, NJ

Hoaglano, Lauren, Grade 5, Eugene Field School, Webb City, MO

Holcomb, Ami, Grade 4, Jefferson School, Taft, CA

Honeycutt, Tina, 11, Chalkville Elementary, Birmingham, AL

Howell, Matt, Grade 6, Freeman School, Haysville, KS

Hudson, Derek, Grade 6, Toledo Middle School, Toledo, WA

Hultman, Kriss, Grade 6, Western Middle School, Parma, MI

Ivy, Julie, Grade 4, Surfside Middle School, Panama City Beach, FL

James, Bethany, Grade 4, Hoxie Grade School, Hoxie, KS

Johnson, Greg, Grade 6, Genoa Public School, Genoa, NE

Johnson, Natalie, Grade 4, Sneads Elementary, Sneads, FL

Johnson, Sam, Grade 4, Teresa Mulvey School, Westbrook, CT

Jones, Janie, Grade 6, Freeman School, Haysville, KS

Kennedy, Luke James, 10, Colonial School, Pelham, NY

Knappenberger, Heather, Grade 5, Sinking Spring Elementary, West Lawn, PA

Koenig, Nicholas, Grade 5, Nazareth Academy, Victoria, TX

Kornitz, Amanda Star, Grade 6, St. Mathew's School, Milwaukee, WI

Lantry, Patrick, 11, Allamuchy Elementary, Allamuchy, NJ

Lawson, Kristee, Grade 4, Unadilla Elementary, Unadilla, GA

Lesser, Elizabeth, Grade 6, Wiesbaden Middle School, APO New York, NY

Lewis, Jason, Grade 5, Maugansville Elementary, Maugansville, MD

Lewis, Karen, Grade 4, Veterans Park School, Ridgefield, CT

Long, Stacy, Grade 5, Saints Peter & Paul School, Waterbury, CT

Macchia, Dina, Grade 6, Louis Armstrong Middle School I.S. 227, East Elmhurst, NY

Marino, Chrissie, Grade 5, Alexandria Middle School, Pittstown, NJ

Martin, Katie, Grade 4, Stella Niagara Educational Park School, Stella Niagara, NY

Matheny, Blake, Grade 4, Veterans Park School, Ridgefield, CT

McBride, Mindy, Grade 6, Quinlan Middle School, Quinlan, TX

McNerney, Kyle, Grade 6, Old County Road School, Smithfield, RI

Meier, Sarah, Grade 5, Christ the King School, Little Rock, AR

Munns, Shannon, Grade 5, Horace Mann Elementary, Sedalia, MO

Nathe, Margarite, Grade 4, St. Anthony School, San Antonio, FL

Nichols, Leslie, Grade 5, Coal Mountain Elementary, Cumming, GA

Norton, Emily, Grade 6, Peterson Elementary, Klamath Falls, OR

Nunez, Sharon, Grade 6, P.S. No. 4, Cliffside Park, NJ

Padilla, Carolina, Grade 6, Southside Elementary, Miami, FL

Perkins, Chrissy, Grade 6, Vernon Elementary, Vernon, AL

Pike, Chris, 11, Chalkville Elementary, Birmingham, AL

Prendergast, Erin, Grade 5, P.S. 225 Seaside School, Rockaway Park, NY

Pruitt, Sean, Grade 6, Cadwallader School, San Jose, CA

Puvalowski, Kristen, Grade 4, St. Mary's School, Ruth, MI

Quezada, Roberto, Grade 6, Modoc Middle School, Alturas, CA

Radich, Jennifer, Grade 6, McKinley School, Lackawanna, NY

Rae, Christina, Grade 4, Teresa Mulvey School, Westbrook, CT

Rasmussen, Nicole, Grade 4, Pioneer Elementary, Colorado Springs, CO

Richardson, Christopher, Grade 4, St. Rose of Lima School, North Wales, PA

Ridgele, Lakesha, Grade 5, Monticello Intermediate, Monticello, AR

Roberts, Nicole, Grade 5, Southeastern Elementary, Bowen, IL

Rogers, Cheryl, Grade 6, Louis Armstrong Middle School I.S. 227, East Elmhurst, NY

Romej, Steven, Grade 4, Village Meadows School, Sierra Vista, AZ

Sabur, Fatin, Grade 6, P.S. No. 4, Cliffside Park, NJ

Sanders, Brianna, Grade 5, Hayward Elementary, Sioux Falls, SD

Santos, Tristan, Grade 4, Balboa Blvd. Elementary, Northridge, CA

Schlesinger, Mitchell, 11, Allamuchy Elementary, Allamuchy, NJ

Schneider, Michelle, Grade 5, Elida Elementary, Elida, OH

Scungio, Alyssa, Grade 5, Stone Hill School, Cranston, RI

Seda, Shannon, Grade 4, Enterprise Elementary, Enterprise, FL

Shorter, Tiffany, Grade 5, East Montgomery Elementary, Clarksville, TN

Soo-Hoo, Sunner, Grade 6, Louis Armstrong Middle School I.S. 227, East Elmhurst, NY

Stalls, James, Grade 5, Walter Bickett School, Monroe, NC

Steen, Monica, Grade 5, Kitzingen American School, APO New York, NY

Steffen, Anna, Grade 4, Selinsgrove Elementary, Selinsgrove, PA

Stock, Sean, Grade 4, Indian Ridge Elementary, Aurora, CO

Storm, Amanda, Grade 5, Eugene Field School, Webb City, MO

Streich, Kaysha, Grade 4, Jefferson School, Taft, CA

Stuck, John, Grade 5, Sinking Spring Elementary, West Lawn, PA

Sullivan, Katie, Grade 5, Flanagan Grade School, Flanagan, IL

Tate, Amanda, 11, Chalkville Elementary, Birmingham, AL

Thomas, Holly, Grade 4, Wellington Elementary, Wellington, TX

Thornton, Nicole, Grade 6, Bowmar Avenue Elementary, Vicksburg, MS

Thornton, Robin, 11, Chalkville Elementary, Birmingham, AL

Treadwell, Jennifer, Grade 5, Jamison Middle School, Pearland, TX

Van de Kamp, Fritz, Grade 4, William Penn Elementary, Salt Lake City, UT

Venet, Eric, 12, Owen-Withee School, Owen, WI

Washington, Natalie, Grade 4, Unadilla Elementary, Unadilla, GA

Weaver, Nicole, Grade 4, C.W. Rice Elementary, Northumberland, PA

Webster, Leslie Ann, Grade 6, Taylor County Elementary, Campbellsville, KY

Wheeler, John, Grade 5, Jamison Middle School, Pearland, TX

Williams, Alonzo, Grade 4, Unadilla Elementary, Unadilla, GA

Wilson, Brad, Grade 6, Hardin Intermediate, Duncanville, TX

Zabinsky, Katie, Grade 4, All Saints Catholic School, Cresson, PA